D1123583

SECRETS OF THE UNEXPLAINED

Extraordinary Events and Oddball Occurrences

by Gary L. Blackwood

BENCHMARK BOOKS

MARSHALL CAVENDISH
NEW YORK

Benchmark Books
Marshall Cavendish Corporation
99 White Plains Road
Tarrytown, New York 10591

Library of Congress Cataloging-in-Publication Data
Blackwood, Gary L.
Extraordinary events and oddball occurrences / Gary L. Blackwood.
p.   cm. — (Secrets of the unexplained)
Includes bibliographical references and index.
Summary: Discusses the details and possible explanations of mysterious events throughout
human history, including strange things falling out of the sky, the teleportation of objects,
and unexplained appearances and disappearances.
ISBN 0-7614-0748-0
1. Parapsychology—Juvenile literature. 2.Curiosities and wonders. [1. Parapsychologyy. 2. Supernatural.
3. Curiosities and wonders.] I. Title. II. Series: Blackwood, Gary L. Secrets of the unexplained.
BF1031.B575 1999   001.9—dc21   98-30261   CIP   AC

Photo Research: Debbie Needleman
Front cover: Michel Tcherevkoff/The Image Bank; Back cover: GK&Vikki Hart/The Image Bank; pages 6, 8, 13,
21: Charles Walker Collection/Stock Montage; pages 10–11, 19, 32, 37, 53, 63: Fortean Picture Library; page
15: Stock Montage; page 16: R.J.A.Rickard/Fortean Picture Library; pages 25, 46–47: UPI/Corbis-Bettmann;
page 27: Mary Evans Picture Library; pages 28–29: Steve Krongard/The Image Bank; page 33: Corbis-
Bettmann; page 35: Janet & Colin Bord/Fortean Picture Library; page 41: Alfred Gescheidt/The Image Bank;
page 44: Grant V. Faint/The Image Bank; page 49: Booth Museum/Fortean Picture Library; page 55: Andrew
Barker/Fortean Picture Library; page 59: Hulton Getty Collection/Liaison International; page 67: Ron
Schaffner/Fortean Picture Library; page 68: Ripley Entertainment/The Image Bank

Printed in Hong Kong

1   3   5   6   4   2

Contents

Introduction

If you watch the news on TV regularly, you might get the idea that the world is a pretty predictable place. There's a very familiar feel to most of the stories. Another politician is involved in a career-threatening scandal? Ho-hum. Another study shows that getting lots of exercise and eating raw veggies is good for your health? Been there, done that. Yet another study reveals that American schoolkids can barely read and write? These items hardly deserve the name "news."

But if you could search diligently through enough newspapers and magazines, occasionally you'd stumble across some news items truly worthy of the title, the sorts of events that make you realize the world is a much weirder and wilder place than the evening news broadcasts let on.

(We're not talking here about such newspapers as the *National Enquirer* and the *Star*, which specialize in the sensational—and often inaccurate—but about papers and journals with a reputation for accuracy.)

You might, for example, come across a story like the one that the *New York World* reported in 1908. A large black dog strolled past

Since ancient times people have reported seeing frogs raining down from the sky.

police detectives, said, "Good morning," then vanished into a green mist. Or you might read about a shower of money from the sky like the one that fell on France in 1957, or a downpour of albino frogs like the one that pelted England in 1987.

You might learn that kangaroos have been sighted in Middle America, or that rocks in Death Valley seem to be moving all by themselves, that a monstrous jellyfish has been seen hovering over the Russian city of Petrozavodsk, or that four huge depressions in an Italian cornfield were the exact shape of a chicken's footprint—but sixteen feet across.

Actual news reports like these were the lifelong obsession of American journalist Charles Hoy Fort. Fort, who was born in 1874, began collecting reports of odd and unexplained events at an early age. By the time he was twenty-three, he'd jotted down and filed some 25,000 of them. Then he decided that "they were not what I wanted" and destroyed them.

In 1916, when he was forty-two, Fort inherited enough money to give up writing for newspapers and go back to exploring them for news of the weird. Day after day for the next sixteen years, Fort pored over newspapers and journals in the New York Public Library and the library of the British Museum in London. He noted curious events on slips of paper and filed the slips in shoe boxes.

Fort felt that science was doing the world a big disservice by ignoring these strange phenomena. He did his best to remedy the situation by compiling his findings in four books: *The Book of the Damned* (published in 1919), *New Lands* (1923), *Lo!* (1931), and *Wild Talents* (1932).

A number of influential writers, including Theodore Dreiser and Booth Tarkington, championed Fort and promoted his books. In 1931, the year before Fort died, novelist Tiffany Thayer founded the Fortean Society to promote the sort of research Fort was doing. Fort, who distrusted organizations, refused to join. He even had to be tricked into attending a banquet the society held in his honor.

For the most part, though, the public ignored his work—until the 1950s, when the "flying saucer" phenomenon (see *Alien Astronauts* in this series) sparked a fascination with the paranormal

Charles Fort originally intended to become a naturalist, but changed his mind because scientists, he said, tended to ignore or discredit everything that did not conform to scientific theory.

that continues to this day. (The term *paranormal* refers to events that conventional science can't explain.)

Modern parapsychologists—researchers who study the paranormal—recognize Fort as a pioneer in the field. In fact, they use the term *Fortean phenomena* to describe a wide range of unexplained events.

All true Fortean phenomena have one thing in common: they're not isolated incidents that occur just once, such as the dog who said, "Good morning." Fort calls events of this kind "marvels." Fortean phenomena are events that have been reported, with similar details, by numerous witnesses in various times and places.

PART ONE

Out
of the
Blue

Falling Fish and Frogs

There are probably more examples of one particular type of Fortean event than any other—the phenomenon known as skyfall. Skyfall is just what the name implies—objects of all sorts raining down from the sky. Sometimes the fall happens during an otherwise ordinary rainstorm. Other times the sky is perfectly clear. At still other times observers have noted a single small dark cloud of red, yellow, or black hovering overhead.

The falling objects themselves come in a mind-boggling variety of types and classifications from the ordinary to the unknown, from apples to alligators, from corn to candy, from snakes to stones to starfish to a jellylike substance known as star rot. No one has yet reported a case in which it was raining cats and dogs.

The two most commonly reported objects in skyfalls are fish and frogs. According to *Australian Natural History* magazine, at least fifty-four fish falls have occurred in that country in the past century. In a remote village in the Central American country of Honduras, a fall of fish is a regular yearly event. At the beginning of each rainy season, villagers gather on a grassy plain outside town, armed with

One of the curious characteristics of skyfalls is their selective nature; most consist solely of objects or creatures of a single type and size.

buckets, baskets, and barrels, ready to scoop up the tens of thousands of three- to four-inch sardines that plummet from the sky. This has been going on for as long as anyone can remember.

In fact, showers of frogs and fish date back almost as far as recorded history. Around A.D. 200 Greek historian Athenaeus wrote of a rain of fish that went on uninterrupted for three days. Athenaeus also recorded a downpour of frogs in such numbers that the people of Paeonia and Dardania "found that all their vessels were filled with them, and the frogs were found to be boiled up and roasted with everything they ate. . . . They could not make use of any water, nor put their feet on the ground for the heaps of frogs that were everywhere."

For as long as such falls have been reported, skeptics have insisted that the fish and frogs couldn't have come from the sky, that they must have appeared on the ground some other way, and people only assumed they fell from above.

Though occasionally fish fall from a cloudless sky, most such falls are accompanied by rain. This led early Roman naturalist Pliny the Elder to theorize that there must be "fish and frog seeds" lying dormant in the soil, and that the rainfall brought them to life.

Later scientists suggested that a heavy rainfall might flush multitudes of frogs from their hiding places in the earth. As for the fish, they might have been left high and dry by a river that overflowed its banks.

It's true that some people who report seeing scads of frogs and fish see them only on the ground. But in plenty of cases witnesses have actually observed the creatures' descent. Many accounts describe the animals bounding off hats and umbrellas, or landing with

Many centuries before Charles Fort began his research, historians and naturalists such as Pliny the Elder were speculating about the nature of skyfalls.

a splat on rooftops or pavement. In 1809 a British army lieutenant in India recalled how dozens of falling fish had lodged in the hats of his men. He emphasized that "they were not *flying fish*, they were dead and falling from the well-known effect of gravity."

Sometimes the fish in skyfalls are alive; but even when they're dead, they're almost always fresh. A number of the fish that deluged Marksville, Louisiana, in 1947 were frozen. They must have raised some nasty bumps on the heads of those unlucky enough to be under them.

When live frogs filled a street in Leicester, Massachusetts, in 1953, naturalists believed they must have hopped there from an over-flowing pond. If that's so, they must have been some terrific hoppers. Hundreds of the frogs were found on rooftops and in rain gutters.

It seems obvious that fish and frogs do, in fact, fall from the sky occasionally. Scientists and scholars who accept this have offered a number of possible explanations. The most popular explanation was first proposed in the sixteenth century by Italian physician Jerome Cardan. According to this theory, the animals are sucked up from some body of water by a waterspout or a tornado, then dropped again several miles away.

This seems like a reasonable enough theory, but it fails to

Though some Fortean scholars suggest that skyfalls originate in some other universe, the objects involved are usually very ordinary, like these fish that rained down on London in 1984.

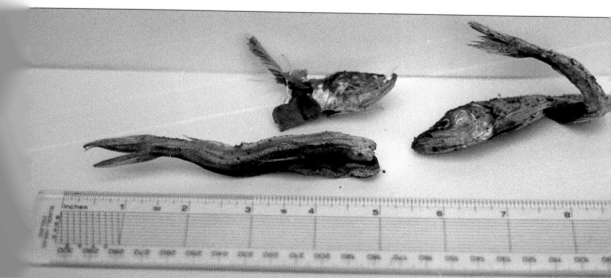

account for some important facts: 1) Falls often take place on clear, still days. 2) The animals are usually deposited on a limited, clearly defined area, not spread out along a path, as a tornado would do. 3) Falls of toads are nearly as common as frog storms, and toads don't live in bodies of water. 4) The falls are nearly always "pure"—that is, they don't contain mud or stones, or plants and other forms of life you'd expect to find if a pond or lake were being emptied. They're almost exclusively fish or frogs or toads, and usually only ones of a single type or size. It's hard to imagine a tornado or waterspout being that picky.

Besides, as Charles Fort wryly pointed out, "It seems to me that anybody who had lost a pond would be heard from."

Snakes, Stones, and Sweets

Frogs and fish aren't the only animals that drop from the sky. In 1855 a cold rain left Fairfax Court House, Virginia, blanketed in what looked like black velvet. Examined closely, the "velvet" proved to be a mass of black bugs the size of pinheads. A bit yucky, but not nearly as alarming as the skyfall that struck Memphis, Tennessee, in 1877 and left behind thousands of foot-long live snakes. Or the deluge of small alligators that fell—not once but twice—on South Carolina in 1943.

The heavens have let loose a vast variety of inanimate (non-living) objects, too. A rain of salt pelted Louisiana in 1867. For nearly a century a town in India has been experiencing the occasional shower of tiny blue-and-green beads, complete with holes for threading.

In 1880 the town of Ozark, Arkansas, was bombarded by thousands of small stones. Six years later Charleston, South Carolina, suffered three similar skyfalls. Some of these stones were as large as hen's eggs, and all were warm to the touch. For about four months in 1921, regular rains of rocks pounded Chico, California; some of them weighed a pound or more.

Most skyfalls are relatively harmless; some are even beneficial. But this steel chain that dropped from the sky over Rock Hill, Missouri, in 1959 could have proven fatal to tractor driver Wallace Baker.

Not all the objects that come out of the blue are as dangerous as stones, snakes, or alligators. Some are actually very welcome, such as the silver coins that sprinkled central Russia during a 1940 storm, or the banknotes that landed in the streets of Limburg, Germany, in 1976.

Sometimes the sky even yields something edible, such as the hundreds of fresh apples that rained down on a family in Lancashire, England, well past apple season. Or Louisiana's 1961 downpour of peaches—which were, unfortunately, green. In 1857 children in Lake County, California, were amazed and delighted by two separate showers of rock candy crystals.

In 1939 a sweet, sticky substance drizzled down on the African country of Angola. A drought had left the local people near starvation, and they eagerly devoured the substance, which fell for days on end. When experts examined the mysterious manna, they determined that it was just what it appeared to be—honey.

Residents of Kentucky weren't quite as grateful for the substance that rained down on them in 1876—flakes of what looked like fresh meat. One opinion was that the flakes must actually be dried particles of nostoc, a kind of freshwater algae. But doctors who examined the meat under microscopes identified it as lung tissue from either humans or horses. Some suggested the flakes had been barfed up by passing buzzards. If so they must have been invisible, and there must have been an awful lot of them, because the meat fall covered an area the size of a football field.

There are so many different sorts of skyfall and the circumstances surrounding them are so varied, it seems unreasonable to expect a single, blanket explanation to cover all of them. When such explanations are offered, they tend either to be full of holes, as the tornado theory is, or to be so theoretical that they seem like pure speculation.

Damon Knight, author of a biography of Charles Fort, suggests

Some supposed skyfalls, such as the skydiving cow pictured in this fifteenth-century woodcut, are hard to swallow. But rains of frogs and fish are so wide-spread and so numerous, they're impossible to dismiss.

that objects could conceivably drop in from some parallel universe, through electromagnetic "channels." A similar theory, based on modern physics, says that there may be other dimensions beyond the three we're used to, and that some sort of fault or "wormhole" could open up between dimensions, letting things leak through.

Charles Fort playfully proposed that hovering high above us is an unseen region he called the Super-Sargasso Sea. There, all sorts of debris are held in suspension, "things from the times of the Alexanders, Caesars and Napoleons of Mars and Jupiter and Neptune; things raised by this earth's cyclones: horses and barns and elephants and flies and dodoes, moas, and pterodactyls." Fort theorized that periodic violent storms shake some of this accumulation loose and it tumbles to the earth.

Fort also proposed another, less frivolous possibility—that the objects might have been transported instantaneously from some other place on earth. He even coined a new word for this theoretical phenomenon, a term that's become part of the language of science fiction: *teleportation*. More about that in part two.

Sky Sounds

Strange objects aren't the only things that come out of the blue. Sometimes the sky also seems to be the source of mysterious sounds, ranging from booms and rumbles to voices to a constant, maddening hum.

Probably the most frequently reported celestial sound is a booming noise that witnesses compare to the firing of cannon. Residents of Comrie, Scotland, have been hearing cannonlike booms since 1597. From 1839 to 1841, over two hundred blasts were reported.

In 1805, during his historic cross-country trek with William Clark, Meriwether Lewis described in his journal a series of sounds precisely like "the discharge of a piece of ordinance [ordnance] of 6 pounds at the distance of three miles." An archaeologist who supervised a dig at one of Lewis and Clark's campsites has also reported hearing the sounds several times.

Lewis wrote of hearing three booms in succession. Some witnesses have noted that the mysterious detonations known as the Barisal Guns, which have been heard in the Ganges Delta of India for over a century, also tend to come in groups of three.

Near Middletown, Connecticut, booming sounds called the Moodus noises have been reported since colonial days, both by the English colonists and by the Native Americans, who called the area Morehemoodus, or "place of noises." Around 1815 the Reverend Henry Chapman wrote that the native peoples believed "the Indian god was angry because the English god intruded upon him, and those [the noises] were the expressions of his displeasure."

Tribes who lived in what is now New York State gave a similar explanation for the noises known as the guns of Seneca Lake. According to legend, the sounds are the angry voice of the warrior Agayenteh, who was slain by the Great Spirit for doing some wrong.

Scientists have claimed that Seneca Lake's "guns" are really bubbles of natural gas escaping from the bottom of the lake and exploding on the surface. This is only one of many natural explanations offered for such sounds. The most obvious one—that someone really was firing cannon—has been ruled out in most cases. So has the possibility of thunder; the sounds nearly always come from a clear, cloudless sky.

The sounds are sometimes attributed to rocks bursting as the earth shifts, or to the crashing of ocean waves, or to sonic booms. But these explanations fit only certain areas or time periods, and celestial booms have been reported from all over the globe for centuries.

Other types of sky sounds are less common, and even more mysterious. For example, there's the "Bug Hum" that plagued much of the population of Kent, England, in the early 1960s. Not everyone could hear the hum, only those who were sensitive to low-

"MYSTERY OF THE DEEP"

Mysterious noises sometimes issue from the ocean as well as from the sky. In the 1960s, scientists were baffled by a series of powerful and unfamiliar sounds that came from the depths and seemed to change position, as though they were emitted by some giant creature.

pitched sounds. Because Kent lies on the ocean, some investigators blamed this sound, too, on the waves.

Another epidemic of humming has been driving residents of the American Southwest batty since 1989 or so. One of the hot spots is Taos, New Mexico, which is hundreds of miles from the nearest ocean. An electronics technician ran tests with vibration detectors and concluded that the noise was caused by seismic slips—small earth movements along fault lines. But the hum is also heard in places where there's no seismic activity.

A gradual increase in industrial noise is another possible culprit, though towns such as Taos are hardly big centers of industry. Even if scientists do track down the source of the sound, they're not likely to be able to fix it, so local residents are learning to cope with the annoyance. "I used to play nature tapes to block out the hum," says a woman in Albuquerque, New Mexico. "Now I'm just used to it."

A few sky sounds seem to be something more than just random noises. In 1899 inventor Nikola Tesla picked up, on his experimental radio, signals with "a clear suggestion of number and order." He believed they were messages from outer space.

In the same year Guglielmo Marconi, another radio pioneer, received "messages from space" that contained the Morse code signal for the letter v. Marconi had been using that signal himself in test transmissions.

In 1963, as astronaut Gordon Cooper was orbiting the earth in a Mercury space capsule, his communications with mission control were interrupted by voices speaking a language that even expert linguists couldn't understand or identify. Later astronauts had the same experience.

German scientist Dr. Hans Bender began investigating a similar phenomenon in 1964—voices that turned up on a tape recording of bird calls. Bender and his associates met with the man who made the recording, a Swede, and did some test recordings of their own. Though everyone involved was careful not to speak during the recording sessions, when the tapes were replayed, faint voices were heard.

Compared to the giant radio telescopes that scan the skies today, the equipment on which Guglielmo Marconi picked up radio signals from space a century ago seems primitive.

The voices were definitely not those of the investigators, yet the words usually paralleled in some way the thoughts going through their minds at the time the recording was made. When the word *Rasmus* was heard on one tape, Dr. Bender observed that, during the recording session, he'd been thinking about a friend named Brigette Rasmus. At a later session one member of Bender's team was suffering from a bad toothache. When the tape was played back, the investigators clearly heard the German words *Zahnarzt, Zahnarzt* (*dentist, dentist*).

PART TWO

Comings
and
Goings

Drop-Ins and Dropouts

In his book *Lo!* Charles Fort suggested that, when "things and materials" appear seemingly out of nowhere, it may be that they're actually being transported from somewhere else by a paranormal force or process he called teleportation.

Occasionally, he felt, this force might even snatch up people unexpectedly from one spot and deposit them in another. This sounds far-fetched but, in fact, it seems as logical an explanation as any for the many appearances and disappearances that have mystified people for hundreds of years.

One of the earliest recorded cases involves a Spanish soldier named Gil Pérez. In 1593 Pérez appeared suddenly outside the governor's palace in Mexico City, looking bewildered and out of place. When authorities questioned him, he revealed that the last thing he remembered was standing guard outside another governor's palace—in Manila, the capital of the Philippines, half a world away. He also mentioned that the governor of the Philippines had died the previous night.

Thinking Pérez was either a liar or a madman, the authorities had him locked up. Two months later a ship arrived from the Philippines with the news that the governor had, indeed, died exactly how and when the man had claimed. What's more, passengers from the ship recognized Pérez and remembered seeing him in Manila the day before he appeared so unexpectedly in Mexico. Pérez was set free and returned to his post in Manila, in a far slower and more mundane manner.

A man who showed up inexplicably in Portugal in the sixteenth century wasn't so lucky. Mere moments before, he said, he'd been in the Portuguese colony of Goa, in India. He had no clear notion of how he came to be back in Portugal, except that he must have been brought there "in the air, in an incredible short time." He was tried by the Catholic Church, found guilty of witchcraft, and burned at the stake.

An apparent teleportation that took place in London in 1871 had a much more comical flavor. A portly woman named Mrs. Guppy, dressed only in a nightgown, was talking with a friend and working on the household budget at her dining table when she abruptly vanished. A moment later she popped up at a séance in a room several miles away, still clutching her account book. "Good God," cried one of those present at the séance, "there's something on my head!"—a pretty mild complaint, considering that Mrs. Guppy weighed two hundred pounds.

Three more recent cases, all very similar, suggest that teleportation may still be at work in the world—and not just on *Star Trek*. In 1968 a couple in Brazil were driving on a honeymoon trip when they

According to Charles Fort, between 1907 and 1913 over three thousand
Londoners disappeared without a trace. Some of them, he speculated, might
have been relocated by a process he called teleportation.

grew drowsy and lost consciousness. When they woke, they found
they'd somehow been transported to Mexico.

 An Argentinean doctor and his wife, on their way home from a
family reunion, drove into a thick cloud of mist and fell asleep. When

they regained consciousness two days later, they were near Mexico City, 4,500 miles away.

A Brazilian sugar merchant was motoring to Uruguay with his wife when they, too, drove into a white cloud. They promptly passed out and came to in—you guessed it—Mexico.

After the writer Ambrose Bierce and a man named Ambrose Small disappeared within a few years of each other, Charles Fort quipped, "Was somebody collecting Ambroses?" If Fort were still alive, it's easy to picture him commenting, "Perhaps Mexico is collecting South Americans." Of course it's possible that all three Latin American incidents are variations of a single incident.

In none of the above cases (except those of the two Ambroses) was there any mystery about where the victims came from or where they ended up, only about how and why the displacement happened. But there are many incidents in which a person appears from somewhere unknown, or disappears to someplace equally unknown.

Twenty years after writing the fictional account of a man who vanished, journalist and author Ambrose Bierce did a disappearing act of his own. Historians suspect he was killed while covering the siege of Ojinaga, during the Mexican Revolution.

Unexplained Appearances

 There are dozens of stories, from several countries and several centuries, of people who turn up in our midst, claiming to have come from some strange land. Two of the most baffling cases took place in England and in Spain; both involved mysterious "green children."

The English account dates from the twelfth century. It tells of a young boy and girl found wandering in a field in the county of Suffolk, crying uncontrollably. They wore "garments of strange color and unknown materials" and their skin had a pronounced greenish tint. They spoke a strange language, and they refused to eat any sort of food except beans.

On that meager diet the boy grew weak and died, but the girl learned to eat more nutritious food. As she regained her health, her skin became pink. When she learned to speak English, she revealed that she came from a country called St. Martin's Land, where there was no sun, only a sort of eternal twilight, and everything was colored green. She and the boy had entered our world, she said, by way of an underground cavern.

The English town of Woolpit, Suffolk, still displays a sign depicting the "green children" who, according to local legend, appeared there under bizarre circumstances in the twelfth century.

Modern scholars tend to dismiss the story as a sort of fairy tale, or to look for some ordinary explanation. One says the children could have been trapped in one of the local flint mines so long they grew unnaturally pale, and might have spoken some dialect unfamiliar to the uneducated farmers of Suffolk.

But William of Newburgh, the medieval scholar who interviewed the witnesses and recorded their version of the incident, wrote, "I was so overwhelmed by the weight of so many competent witnesses that I have been compelled to believe."

The account that comes from Spain is so similar as to seem like a retelling of the English story—except that the events took place some seven hundred years later. In this version a boy and girl with green skin and almond-shaped eyes emerged from a cave near Banjos in 1887. They spoke no Spanish and wouldn't eat the food that was offered to them. The boy died but the girl lived on for five more years, long enough to learn Spanish and to tell of a sunless land from which she'd been swept away by a whirlwind. (Could L. Frank Baum, author of *The Wonderful Wizard of Oz*, have been familiar with this story?)

As the world's population has increased, so has the number of reports of people showing up from parts unknown—or at least known only to them. A man found wandering near Frankfurt an der Oder in Germany in 1850 claimed to hail from a place called Laxaria, in the country of Sakria. Neither can be found on any map of our world.

Another fellow arrested for vagrancy in Paris in 1905 spoke a language no one could identify, but managed to communicate that he came from the unheard-of country of Lisbian. And then there's the

Perhaps the most celebrated "wild man" was a teenage boy known as Kaspar Hauser, who turned up in Nuremberg, Germany, in 1828. He could not speak coherently and seemed frightened by ordinary objects. His death five years later was equally mysterious.

stranger who appeared in a town in New Jersey in 1928, insisting that he was from Mars.

Not all strange visitors are so sure of where they came from. Many are totally befuddled and disoriented, and unable to identify themselves. Nineteenth-century newspapers dubbed such incoherent individuals "wild men."

According to the *New York Times*, five "wild men" and a "wild girl" suddenly materialized in a street in Connecticut in January 1888. All six were suffering from concussion—jarring of the brain caused by a blow or fall.

In the winter of 1904–1905 at least ten wild men turned up in different parts of England. One reportedly spoke an unknown language and carried a book full of indecipherable writing.

The years 1920–1923 saw another spate of mysterious strangers. A total of six people were found at various times wandering in or near the small town of Romford in Essex, England, unable to tell who they were or where they'd come from.

What became of all these lost souls? Newspaper reports indicate that several of them were declared insane and committed to an asylum or mental hospital. But for the most part there's no record of whether or not these displaced persons were ever able to account for themselves.

Though there's no way of knowing the origins of those green children and wild men, it stands to reason they must have come from somewhere—unless, that is, you buy a theory proposed by Robert Rickard, former editor of the newsletter *Fortean Times*. Rickard suggests that "some of the people in this world of ours may not be real in the same way that we think of ourselves as real." In other words there may be phantom beings who come and go among us, similar to the ghostlike entities called *tulpas* that Tibetan mystics occasionally create through long, intense concentration. (See *Spooky Spectres* in this series.)

There's nothing ghostlike, though, about most of these immigrants from elsewhere. They eat, they carry on conversations, they can be physically restrained.

If there are, in fact, flesh-and-blood people appearing inexplicably around the world, it seems logical to assume that people must be disappearing from somewhere else in roughly equal numbers.

And that does seem to be the case.

Unexplained Disappearances

 If we use the term *disappear* loosely, then thousands of people disappear without a trace each year. In the city of London alone, an average of seven people *per day* go missing.

Of course most of those people haven't literally vanished. They've been abducted, or been murdered or killed by accident, or they may have just run off. Occasionally, people even lapse into what's called a fugue state, which can last for months or years. In this state, a person loses all knowledge of his or her former life and takes on a whole new identity.

But there are also a surprising number of stories of people who are in full view of witnesses one moment and, the next moment, are simply gone.

A servant named Diderici, who was imprisoned in Prussia

Some physicists speculate that one or more other dimensions exist alongside ours, and that objects or people may occasionally cross the boundaries between the dimensions.

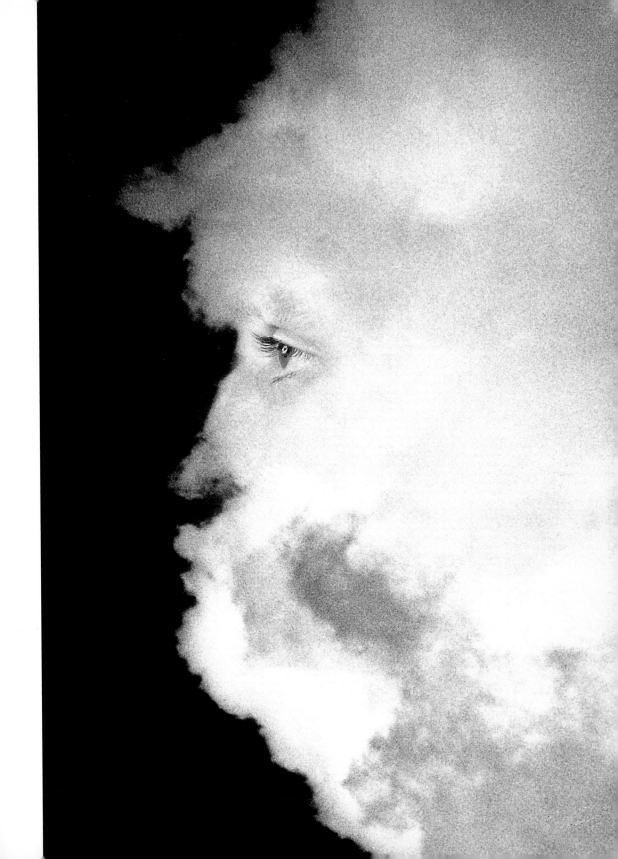

in 1815 for impersonating his master, made a very unusual escape. As he was shuffling across the prison's exercise yard, shackled in chains, he suddenly began to fade away before the eyes of his fellow prisoners and their guards. Within seconds he was totally invisible, and his shackles clanked uselessly to the ground.

In 1873 an English shoemaker, James Worson, bet his friends that he could run to Coventry, eight miles away, and back home without stopping. He lost the bet, but his friends never collected, because Worson vanished. In their report to the police, the three friends swore that, after following Worson in a horse-drawn cart for several miles, they saw the runner stumble, pitch forward with a cry, and then just disappear.

Or so the story goes. The Worson incident has been recounted many times, always with the same details, but no one has produced conclusive evidence that it happened, or that Worson was a real person.

Several other accounts of missing men are so similar to one another that they almost have to be versions of a single story. But what the original story was, no one knows. Probably the earliest version tells of an Alabama farmer named Orion Williamson who, in 1854, set out across a field to fetch his horses. Before the eyes of his wife and child and two neighbors, Williamson vanished.

A virtual duplicate of the incident supposedly took place in 1880 in Tennessee. This time the farmer's name was David Lang. Again the disappearance was witnessed by the wife and two neighbors. The tale was recounted by Lang's daughter years later. In 1885 the *New York Sun* reported a copycat disappearance in Virginia, involving a farmer named Isaac Martin.

As with the tale of the running shoemaker, there's no hard evidence to support the stories. Some scholars think all three versions are based not on actual events but on fictional ones. The most likely source is an 1893 short story by Ambrose Bierce—the writer who later "disappeared" himself—titled "The Difficulty of Crossing a Field." But of course Bierce wrote his story long after the events were supposed to have happened, which leads others to believe that he based the story on a true incident, perhaps the Orion Williamson episode.

An equal measure of confusion surrounds the tale of sixteen-year-old Charles Ashmore of Illinois who, in November 1878, reportedly went to the well to fetch water and never returned. His family followed his footsteps in the snow, but the prints ended halfway to the well. For days afterward Charles's dismayed mother could hear his disembodied voice calling for help, but she had no idea where to find him.

The same details surface in the story of eleven-year-old Oliver Larch of Indiana, who met an identical fate on Christmas Eve 1889, and that of Oliver Thomas of Wales, who vanished in 1909, also on Christmas Eve. It seems obvious that all three accounts are variations of a single incident, but whether it was a real incident or an invented one is anybody's guess.

No one actually saw what happened to Ashmore or Larch or Thomas. They saw only the circumstantial evidence—the footprints that abruptly stopped. That's true of most mysterious disappearances. The victim's fate is unknown. The only certainty is that he or she is inexplicably gone.

A trail of footprints that simply stops is a prominent feature in several stories of disappearing people.

Take the case of Sherman Church, which was reported in the January 5, 1900, issue of the *Chicago Tribune*. Church, an employee of Augusta Mills in Battle Creek, Michigan, ran inside the company's mill one day and never came out again. The mill was pulled practically to pieces and every foot of the surrounding countryside was combed, but no sign of the missing man was ever found.

In 1924 two British airmen flying a reconnaissance mission in the Middle East landed in a remote stretch of desert and were never heard from again. The following day searchers found the plane, which was in good working order. But they found no trace of the two fliers except their footprints in the sand. The prints led away from the aircraft for about forty yards, then simply stopped.

A double disappearance like this is rare. Even rarer are cases in which a whole group of people seem to have been plucked off the face of the earth.

It seems incredible that the French army could lose 650 of its best men, but in 1858 that's just what happened. The ill-fated troops were sent to put down a riot in Saigon, in Southeast Asia, but they never showed up in that city. Their progress could be traced to within fifteen miles of their destination, but where they got to after that, no one has a clue.

In 1930 trapper Joe Labelle paid one of his regular visits to an Inuit (Eskimo) village in Canada's Northwest Territories. He found that the village's entire population of about thirty men, women, and children, plus their dogs, were unaccountably gone, leaving all their possessions behind. When authorities investigated, they found no tracks leading from the village and no signs of foul play.

It's not all that hard to imagine becoming irretrievably lost in the jungles of Southeast Asia or the sands of a Middle Eastern desert, or on the vast tundra of northwestern Canada. But people also disappear in far less remote areas of the earth. In 1990 eighty-eight bird-watchers took a ferry to the tiny island of Eynhallow, off the coast of Scotland. Two of them never returned. The police and coast guard combed the island with heat-seeking equipment, but found no trace of the missing pair. Ironically, Eynhallow is known in Scottish legend as "the vanishing isle."

vil

PART THREE

Animal Anomalies

Ancient Amphibians

Aside from the dog who said, "Good morning," not much has been written about animals disappearing. But there's a real wealth of reports of animals appearing in totally unexpected places.

When a living thing or an inanimate object is discovered in a place where it doesn't logically belong, scientists call it an anomaly. Sometimes an animal is considered an anomaly because it's in a country where it's not normally found. Other times an animal that scientists have labeled extinct suddenly proves otherwise.

The most astounding sort of anomaly, though, is an animal that's been encased in a chunk of coal or stone for ages, then emerges still living and breathing. Most of these specimens are frogs or toads. There are hundreds of reports of these "living fossils" from as far back as the twelfth century. William of Newburgh, the same scholar who chronicled the history of the green children, thought that such creatures must have been placed there by the Devil.

A toad that was freed from a block of limestone in England in 1865 was "full of vivacity," but had some trouble breathing because

Though the man who donated this specimen to a museum in Brighton, England, was a known perpetrator of hoaxes, many reports of entombed toads come from reliable witnesses.

its mouth seemed to be sealed shut. It did make a barking noise through its nostrils. At first it was deathly pale, but gradually its color darkened. A local geologist guessed that the rock in which the toad was found was at least six thousand years old. Anyone who doubted that the toad had actually been entombed had only to examine the broken limestone. In it was a cavity the exact size and shape of the animal's body.

In 1901 a man in Rugby, England, was poking the coal on his fire when one lump of coal broke open. Inside was a living toad, so pale it was almost transparent. The man rescued it. Though it apparently had no mouth, the animal survived another five weeks.

In 1982, as workers on a New Zealand railroad were digging through rock twelve feet underground, they uncovered a live frog. Later in the day they came upon a second one.

In several rather heartless experiments toads have been deliberately sealed in stone and mortar to test their ability to stay alive. An Oxford professor of mineralogy who entombed twenty-four toads in 1825 and uncovered them a year later found that almost half were still alive and well. In 1897 a man in Texas laid up a live toad inside the walls of a courthouse that was under construction. When the building was demolished thirty-one years later, the toad, nicknamed Old Rip (presumably after Rip van Winkle), seemed none the worse for his long hibernation, and went on to live for another year.

Frogs and toads aren't the only animals that have been rescued from stone coffins. Digging deep in a chalk quarry in 1818, an American geologist came upon three newts of an extinct species. When he set them in the sun, they began to move. He placed the liveliest one in a pond, where it abruptly darted away and out of sight.

Probably the most fantastic living fossil of all time was unearthed in 1856, by workers digging a railway tunnel in France. When they split open a limestone boulder, a huge and startling shape tumbled out, fluttered a pair of leathery wings, and croaked—first literally and then in the more final sense. When examined, the creature proved to have a ten-foot wingspan, long talons, sharp teeth, and thick oily skin. A paleontology student identified it as a pterodactyl, a "flying dinosaur" that had been extinct for 65 million years. The cavity it came from was molded in the shape of the creature's body.

Science offers two possible explanations for the phenomenon of entombed animals. The first explanation assumes that the people who claim to have discovered such anomalies were either lying or mistaken. Perhaps, the skeptics say, the animals were just hidden nearby and only appeared to have hopped from inside the rock. It's hard to imagine, though, where a ten-foot pterodactyl would hide, or how it got there to begin with, or why there just happened to be an indentation in the rock that fit the animal like a glove.

A second theory assumes that such animals actually were entombed, and speculates that the rock contained tiny cracks through which air, water, and food could have seeped, keeping the animal alive. If the rock was limestone, the cracks could later have filled with dissolved lime, which then hardened and made the rock solid and seamless. It's not clear how the animal is supposed to have survived after that happened.

Not Exactly Extinct

When that rockbound pterodactyl drew its final breath in 1856, everyone assumed it was the last of its kind. But since then some naturalists have begun to wonder if the species is as far gone as they thought.

For many years the people of Africa have been telling stories of a flying reptile called a *kongamato*. About 1920 a British official passed a picture of a pterodactyl around to the native people, who unanimously declared it the spitting image of the kongamato.

In 1974 a British expedition reported seeing a pterodactyl-like creature in Kenya. The following year a group of Americans spotted a similar creature over a swamp in Namibia. German settlers in Namibia have also reportedly sighted a "flying snake" with a thirty-foot wingspan.

Africa isn't the only place where winged reptiles turn up. At least three reports have come out of Texas in recent years. In 1982 an ambulance technician driving near Los Fresnos saw a huge birdlike shape swoop down from the sky. It had a thin body covered not with feathers but with grayish skin, and a wingspan of five or six feet.

It seems inconceivable that a creature thought to have vanished 65 million years ago could still exist somewhere. And yet such things happen. In 1938 a fish species called the coelacanth, considered extinct for 60 million years, was discovered swimming off the coast of Africa.

Not all anomalous animals have been out of circulation quite that long. In Britain wild boars were considered wiped out by the end of the nineteenth century. Then in 1976 a careless driver ran one down on a forest road in Scotland. Scientists were sure the last of the woolly rhinoceroses had died off fifty years ago. But in 1986 a small group of the rhinos was discovered in a remote valley in Southeast Asia.

The most famous example of a "living fossil" is the coelacanth, an ancient species of fish thought to be extinct until fishermen caught one near the island of Madagascar.

Out-of-Place Animals

Almost as alarming as seeing an animal that by all accounts no longer exists is seeing one that by all rights shouldn't be where it is—especially when the out-of-place animal is distinctly dangerous.

Floridians might expect to see an alligator now and again, but residents of Detroit, Michigan, definitely don't. Yet a sizable gator was caught roaming the streets of that city in 1960. In 1980 there were three separate sightings of a crocodile on a highway in Lancashire, England. In Wales a twelve-year-old girl was so delighted with the dead crocodile she found in her backyard that she lugged it to school. Health officials took it away.

For the past thirty years lions, leopards, and pumas—referred to by Fortean researchers as Alien Big Cats (ABCs) when the animals are outside their normal territory—have been stalking about Great Britain. Sightings on the Isle of Wight go back a full century. In the past ten years there have been three hundred reports from that island alone. In 1987 an Asian leopard was trapped and shot there.

Another leopard was shot by a farmer in Devon in 1988. One

Sightings of wild cats of various descriptions have been on the rise in Great Britain for the last thirty years. This fierce-looking specimen was shot in Scotland in 1983.

particularly nasty ABC, dubbed the Beast of Inkberrow, has been seen over thirty times. In 1993 it attacked a veterinarian and left deep claw marks across her ribs.

A catlike creature called the Beast of Exmoor was held responsible for a rash of livestock deaths in the 1980s. The British army mounted a cat hunt, but never succeeded in catching the beast.

One researcher blames Britain's big cat population on wealthy sixteenth-century landowners with a taste for exotic pets. Undoubtedly some of their captive cats escaped, and some may have produced wild offspring.

It's harder to come up with a good explanation for the dozens of kangaroos that have been turning up in the United States for the past hundred years. One of the earliest sightings took place in New Richmond, Wisconsin, in 1899, during a tornado. A Mrs. Glover swore she'd seen a kangaroo spring through her backyard. The Gollmar Circus was in town that week, but the circus management denied owning such an animal.

In 1949 a Greyhound bus driver in Grove City, Ohio, nearly ran down another kangaroo. There was a virtual epidemic of kangaroo encounters throughout the Midwest in the 1970s. One of the most comical involved two Chicago police officers who cornered a wayward kangaroo in an alley and tried to handcuff it. The five-foot animal screamed and kicked violently. In return the angry cops punched it in the head. Before reinforcements could arrive, the kangaroo slipped away and bounded off. The following day a Chicago paper ran the headline KEYSTONE KOPS GO ON KANGAROO KAPER.

No one has managed to capture one of the mysterious marsupials alive. A Wisconsin man did snap a clear picture of a kangaroo sitting by the roadside. And in 1981 a man drove into a diner in Tulsa, Oklahoma, with a dead kangaroo in the bed of his pickup. He'd come upon two of the animals in the road, and struck one with his truck. Two police officers took a look and confirmed that the dead animal was without a doubt a kangaroo.

Like the Alien Big Cats, these alien marsupials could conceivably be descendants of animals that escaped from captivity long ago. It's also been suggested that they're not actual kangaroos but a separate species that's native to North America and has somehow, like the wild boar and woolly rhino, managed to keep its existence a secret.

Cryptic Creatures

 It would be startling to see fish or frogs fall from the sky or a kangaroo hop across the lawn. And it would be downright scary to be out for a stroll and come upon an alligator, a leopard, or a lion.

But in cases like these the witnesses at least knew what it was they were seeing. Imagine if you will, encountering some creature that defies classification, that's unlike anything you've ever seen or read about.

In addition to a wealth of inexplicable events, the world of Fortean phenomena has its share of unknown entities. Some are merely mystifying. Some are truly terrifying.

One of the scariest was an elusive, humanlike figure that first appeared around 1837, startling the citizens of southwest London by bounding across their paths like a man on a supercharged pogo stick. His incredibly high leaps earned him the nickname Spring-Heeled Jack.

In February of the following year, Jack's actions grew more alarming. He accosted a young woman named Jane, ripping her dress and

The strange and terrifying figure known as Spring-Heeled Jack made frequent appearances in nineteenth-century London, and in the popular literature of the day.

clawing her face and neck. Jane's sister heard her screams and went for help, but before anyone could arrive, Jack sprang away into the night.

According to Jane's description, Jack wore "a kind of helmet and a tight-fitting white costume. . . . His face was hideous, his eyes were like balls of fire. His hands had great claws, and he vomited blue and white flames."

Though this description sounds fanciful, it was repeated with little variation by dozens of witnesses over the next sixty-six years—and not just in London but throughout England. The army set traps for Jack, and angry townspeople shot at him, but always he laughed and melted away into the dark.

The bounding bogeyman was last seen in England in 1904, leaping through the streets of Liverpool. But nearly fifty years later three residents of Houston, Texas, saw a "huge shadow" spring into a nearby pecan tree. The form perched there long enough for the witnesses to note that it was a tall man in a black cape and skintight pants. Then, like Spring-Heeled Jack, he "just melted away."

No one has ever explained who or what Spring-Heeled Jack was. In illustrations from the period Jack matches most people's concept of what the Devil looks like. The term *Devil* has been applied, though, to several other strange beings. One of these was never actually seen. Witnesses saw only its tracks, which were dubbed the Devil's footprints.

The true nature of the creature (or creatures) that left the Devil's footprints is still being debated, even though the incident took place well over a century ago. On the morning of February 9, 1855, people throughout south Devon in southwest England discovered a line of odd-looking tracks in the snow. The tracks led unbroken for over a hundred miles, over fourteen-foot stone walls, over the roofs of barns and houses, over ricks of hay and the tops of wagons, through six-inch drainpipes. When the tracks came to the Exe River, almost two miles wide, they stopped and then took up again on the opposite shore.

The prints were uniformly four inches long, two and three-quarter inches wide, and shaped like a horseshoe. But no horse alive could have made them, for the prints were laid down in a single straight line, one in front of the other, and were only eight inches apart.

As the snow melted a bit, indentations appeared in some of the tracks, giving rise to the rumor that they'd been made by cloven hooves like those attributed to the Devil. Alarmed citizens with dogs, guns, and pitchforks set out to track down the cloven-hoofed menace. "As might be expected," the *London Times* reported, "the party returned as they went."

Over the next month the story spread throughout England. Newspapers were bombarded with letters from scientists, clergymen, and ordinary citizens claiming to have the definitive explanation of how the Devil's footprints were formed—though very few had actually seen the tracks.

Naturalist Richard Owen considered badgers the likely culprits. The Reverend G. M. Musgrave suggested that kangaroos reportedly on the loose from a private zoo had made the marks. Other suspects included giant leaping rats, swans, camels, penguins, otters, toads, and even a mythical animal called a unipede. Naturally some suspected that the whole thing was a hoax—forgetting that the hoaxer would have had to squeeze through a six-inch pipe, leap high walls at a single bound, and swim a freezing two-mile-wide river.

Letters from two readers pointed out that similar mysterious tracks had been reported in Poland and on desolate Kerguelen Island in the south Indian Ocean.

Since none of the proposed solutions seem to fit the facts, modern scholars have concluded that the prints were made by a variety of animals. Why, then, did they all look the same? Investigator Joe Nickell says that a phenomenon psychologists call contagion may have been at work. The power of suggestion could have led the people of Devon to misinterpret what they saw, to assume that all the tracks were made by a single creature.

Scottish explorer James Alan Rennie came up with a plausible theory that doesn't involve animals at all, but that does account for the way the tracks seemed to surmount every obstacle. When Rennie observed a row of impressions being created in the snow by large, isolated raindrops, he concluded that rain might fall from just one edge of a rain cloud, leaving a straight trail that could be mistaken for an animal's tracks.

On January 17, 1909, residents of New Jersey and Pennsylvania also woke to find a maze of hoofprints in the snow, covering an area of over forty square miles. This time, though, the creature considered responsible for the tracks was sighted numerous times.

A Pennsylvania postmaster who observed the "Jersey Devil" described it as having a head with curled horns like a ram's, long thin wings, and short legs. It uttered a "mournful and awful call—a

This likeness of the flying creature known as the Jersey Devil, drawn from a witness's description, appeared in the Philadelphia Evening Bulletin *soon after the 1909 sightings.*

combination of a squawk and a whistle." A police officer fired at the bizarre form several times, but missed.

In 1926 the Jersey Devil terrified two ten-year-old boys, who described it as a "flying lion." It reappeared in 1930 in a New Jersey cornfield, and again in 1932, prompting citizens to mount a full-scale—and unsuccessful—armed hunt for the beast.

Scientists have offered several possible explanations for the strange sightings. The unimaginative suspected that people were seeing nothing more unusual than a sandhill crane that had lost its way while migrating south from Canada. The more daring theorized that it was a pterodactyl that had escaped extinction. The skeptical chalked it all up to mass hysteria, a phenomenon similar to contagion.

One writer has traced the origins of the Jersey Devil to a 1906 stunt devised by Norman Jefferies, the publicity manager of the Arch Street Museum in Philadelphia, to generate interest in the museum. Jefferies spread rumors of a flying fiend, spooking much of the local populace. Then he created and displayed a creature that matched his story, by strapping a pair of bronze wings onto the body of a live imported kangaroo and painting the animal with green stripes.

It's very possible, though, that Jefferies didn't actually create the Jersey Devil legend, but only capitalized on it. After all, reports of a strange airborne animal in the Pennsylvania-New Jersey area go back much farther than 1906—in fact, back to a time when Native Americans made up most of the area's population.

Another flying monster that newspaper reporters called Mothman (after a *Batman* villain) gets around a lot more than the Jersey Devil. It's been spotted in places as far apart as Washington, Texas, New York, and England, by at least a hundred witnesses.

The most concentrated batch of sightings took place in 1966 and 1967 in the Ohio River Valley of West Virginia. The creature turned up most often near or after dark, making it difficult to see.

Witnesses who saw it on the ground described it as a gray form five to seven feet tall and broader than a man. Its legs were humanlike, but it walked with a curious halting shuffle. Some witnesses saw it unfold a pair of huge batlike wings.

It had no distinct head, but at the top of its body was a pair of large, round, glowing red eyes that, according to one witness, "looked like bicycle reflectors." When the beast flew, it did so without flapping its wings, and it made a strange high-pitched sound described by some as a mechanical hum. Others said it was like "the squeak of a mouse" or a tape recording played at high speed.

When Mothman soared near one witness, the man's hunting dog snarled and took off after the beast. The hound never returned. All its master found the next morning were the dog's tracks, running in a circle.

A biologist at West Virginia University dragged out the sandhill crane theory again, but all the witnesses, when shown pictures of a sandhill crane, saw no resemblance between it and the creature they'd seen.

In any case, the sandhill crane explanation hardly accounts for the feeling of terror that came over those who encountered Mothman. "I've never had that feeling before," said one man, "a weird kind of fear" that "gripped you and held you."

The Ohio River Valley has been visited periodically by another sort of strange and sinister being—an amphibious one. Early one morning in May 1955, a driver near Loveland, Ohio, spotted three grotesque "reptile men" alongside the road. He stopped his car and observed them for several minutes. The three bore a family resemblance to the star of the movie *Creature from the Black Lagoon*, which had been in theaters the year before. They had wide froglike mouths and wrinkled bald heads.

The following August a woman swimming in the Ohio River was seized by a clawlike hand and pulled under the water. She struggled free and swam to shore, to find deep scratches and a palm-shaped green stain on her knee.

In 1972 two Loveland police officers watched a four-foot, frog-faced form with leathery skin leap over a guardrail and scramble toward the Little Miami River. Two weeks later one of the officers spotted the reptile man again and took an ineffectual shot at it. A local farmer reported seeing a similar creature. In 1975 there were multiple reports of a giant lizard that walked on two legs in the vicinity of Louisville, Kentucky.

The lizard men didn't confine themselves to the Midwest, though. In 1958 a California man in a car was attacked by a creature with gills and scales; it left long scratches on his windshield. The man claimed he proceeded to drive over the creature, but apparently no body was ever found. The following evening a monster of the same description jumped from the bushes at another passing motorist.

In two separate incidents in 1972, people lounging by a lake in British Columbia were set upon by a silvery, scaly, humanlike form that emerged from the water. One of the witnesses suffered cuts on his hand from sharp points on the lizard man's head. The following summer New Jersey residents encountered a large being they described as a cross between a man and an alligator.

No one has come up with a convincing theory about what these

The leathery-skinned "Loveland Frogman" was supposedly sighted at least three times in the space of two weeks. One witness was so badly spooked by the creature that he tried to shoot it.

If Charles Fort accomplished nothing else, he at least demonstrated that extraor-dinary events can take place in the most ordinary places, and that it's wise to keep our eyes and our minds open.

reptile men might be. There's always the possibility of a hoax but, considering the damage the creatures have inflicted, the hoaxer would have to have a deranged sense of humor, not to mention some pretty heavy-duty fake claws.

When you're dealing with newspaper reports of Fortean phenomena, particularly those from a century ago, there's always some chance that a hoax is being perpetrated not by witnesses but by the newspaper reporter.

In the nineteenth century journalists were not above inventing sensational events and fabricating facts in order to boost their paper's circulation, or to make more money for themselves. One of the worst such culprits was Louis Stone, a young reporter from Winsted, Connecticut. In the late 1800s Stone earned the nickname the Winsted Liar after selling a whole string of totally bogus stories to New York newspapers.

His first flimflam involved a "wild man" supposedly seen roaming the woods near Winsted. He went on to tell convincing tales of such oddities as a harelipped cat that whistled "Yankee Doodle," a watch that was swallowed by a cow and kept wound up by the force of the animal's breathing, and a tree that grew baked apples.

The papers' editors knew the stories were lies, but printed them anyway because they were so popular. Much of the public never doubted the truth of the stories because they were, after all, printed in black and white.

In 1833 a reporter for the *New York Sun* kept readers spellbound with fictitious descriptions of life on the moon, as observed through a telescope in South Africa. Poet Eugene Field regularly filled his column in the *Chicago Daily News* with "facts" that were patently false. In 1844 master of the macabre Edgar Allan Poe published a gripping account of a transatlantic balloon flight that, unfortunately, never took place.

Though most newspapers today are more conscientious about checking their facts, it obviously isn't wise to believe everything you read. Still, when enough people in enough different places claim that they saw fish fall from the sky, or heard invisible cannon, or saw a crocodile—or something even weirder—in their backyard, it may be safe to assume that there's something out of the ordinary going on.

All his life Charles Fort railed against science because it tried so hard to ignore or to explain away anything out of the ordinary. And it seems the situation hasn't changed much. Some scientists do accept the existence of the paranormal; a few even study it. But researchers Derek and Julia Parker complain that "many scientists take the view that if a phenomenon cannot be scientifically tested and explained, then it cannot exist."

Science is a valuable tool, but there are a lot of things in this world that it can't quite get a grip on, that no one can satisfactorily explain yet. That doesn't necessarily mean we should scoff at or ignore those things.

After all, isn't it the extraordinary events and the oddball occurrences that make life so varied and so fascinating? As Albert Einstein once said, "The most beautiful thing we can experience is the mysterious. It is the source of all true art and science."

Glossary

albino: A term used to describe a person or animal with white skin and pink eyes, due to a lack of pigment.

amphibious: Able to live both on land and in water.

anomaly: An object or animal that's discovered in a time or place where scientists wouldn't expect to find it.

Bierce, Ambrose (1842–1914): American journalist best known for his macabre short stories and his witty, cynical book *The Devil's Dictionary*. In 1913 Bierce went south to report on the Mexican Revolution and was never heard from again.

concussion: A temporary brain injury caused by the shock of a blow or fall; the victim can suffer headaches, memory loss, or unconsciousness.

contagion: A phenomenon in which an idea spreads like a contagious disease, causing people to interpret facts in a way that fits that idea. For example, when news of a UFO sighting spreads, people tend to see any strange object in the skies as a "flying saucer."

Dreiser, Theodore (1871–1945): American novelist, author of *An American Tragedy*, considered by some critics one of the greatest American novels.

Einstein, Albert (1879–1955): Nobel Prize–winning German-American physicist whose theories of relativity revolutionized modern physics.

fugue state: A psychiatric term for a rare state in which a subject loses all knowledge of his or her identity and takes on a new identity. When the subject recovers, all memory of that new identity vanishes.

Isle of Wight: An English county that occupies an island off the south coast of England.

Marconi, Guglielmo (1874–1937): Italian inventor of the wireless telegraph. Marconi shared the 1909 Nobel Prize for physics.

marsupial: A type of mammal that carries its newborn babies in a pouch, or *marsupium*.

nostoc: A colony of freshwater algae, consisting of interwoven threads of plant material embedded in a jellylike substance.

paleontology: The branch of science that studies prehistoric life.

Philippines: An independent nation made up of eleven large islands and thousands of smaller islands that lie five hundred miles off the mainland of Southeast Asia.

Poe, Edgar Allan (1809–1849): American fiction writer, poet, and literary critic whose stories "The Tell-Tale Heart" and "The Pit and the Pendulum" are considered classics of the horror genre.

Prussia: A region in Europe on the southeast coast of the Baltic Sea. It's now part of Germany, but in the eighteenth century it was a separate kingdom with its capital at Berlin.

pterodactyl: One of several kinds of flying reptiles, or pterosaurs, that lived during the late Jurassic and Cretaceous periods, 65 million to 160 million years ago.

sandhill crane: A North American bird, gray in color, with a long neck and legs and a six- to seven-foot wingspan.

séance: A meeting in which a spiritualist, or medium, tries to contact spirits of the dead.

seismic slips: Movements of the earth that occur along a fracture, or fault, and are too small to produce noticeable earthquake activity.

sonic boom: A loud noise caused by the shock wave a jet airplane produces when it flies faster than the speed of sound.

Tarkington, Booth (1869–1946): Indiana-born novelist and playwright who won Pulitzer Prizes for his books *The Magnificent Ambersons* and *Alice Adams*.

teleportation: The unexplained and instantaneous transfer of an object or person from one place to another.

Tesla, Nikola (1856–1943): Croatian-American electrician and inventor who developed the alternating-current motor.

tulpa: An independent entity created by concentrated and disciplined thought.

To Learn More about Fortean Phenomena

BOOKS-NONFICTION

Fuchs, Carol A. *Disappearances*. Mankato, MN: Capstone, 1991. Only partly about actual disappearances. Also discusses lost civilizations, the Bermuda Triangle, and UFO abductions. Color photos.

Gunning, Thomas G. *Unexplained Mysteries*. New York: Dodd, Mead, 1983. Easy-to-read, accurate accounts of nine "strange happenings," including the Devil's footprints. Photos and drawings.

O'Neill, Catherine. *Amazing Mysteries of the World*. Washington, D.C.: National Geographic, 1983. Lavishly illustrated look at a wide range of mysteries from the Bermuda Triangle to black holes.

Powell, Jillian. *Mysteries of the Supernatural*. Brookfield, CT: Copper Beech, 1996. Heavily illustrated. A quick, simple overview of a number of aspects of the unexplained: UFOs, ghosts, paranormal powers, strange creatures.

Wulffson, Don L. *Amazing True Stories*. New York: Cobblehill, 1991. Scads of short tales that run the gamut of the weird and wacky, from disappearances to levitation to a tidal wave of molasses.

ORGANIZATIONS

International Fortean Organization (INFO), P.O. Box 367, Arlington, VA 22210-0367. Scientists and scholars from twenty countries, all concerned with "unusual scientific discoveries." Speakers' bureau (furnishes names of experts who lecture on the paranormal), library, publishes *INFO Journal*, annual FortFest conference.

Society for the Investigation of the Unexplained, Box 265, Little Silver, NJ 07739. Collects and reviews reports of unexplained phenomena of all kinds. Speakers' bureau, library, quarterly journal.

ONLINE INFORMATION*

http://www.research.umbc.edu/~frizzell/info
Home page of the International Fortean Organization (see above).

http://www.knowledge.co.uk/frontiers/sourcebook.htm
Home page of the Sourcebook Project. Offers books for sale on natural phenomena and various anomalies.

http://www.users.cloud9.net/~patrick/anomalist/Fort1.htm
The Anomalist Site, an online magazine. A potpourri of information, commentaries, and letters on Fortean phenomena, quotes from Charles Fort.

http://www.forteantimes.com/
The *Fortean Times* online. A British magazine devoted to reporting all sorts of odd phenomena, much of it trivial.

*Websites change from time to time. For additional on-line information, check with the media specialist at your local library.

Index

Page numbers for illustrations are in boldface

Notes

Quotations in this book are from the following sources:

Page 7 "they were not": *Bizarre Phenomena* by the Editors of *Reader's Digest* (Pleasantville, NY: Reader's Digest, 1992), p. 21.

Page 14 "found that all": *Mysteries of the Unexplained* by the Editors of Reader's Digest (Pleasantville, NY: Reader's Digest, 1982), p. 185.

Page 15 "They were not flying": *Strange Phenomena: A Sourcebook of Unusual Natural Phenomena* compiled by William R. Corliss (Glen Arm, MD: Sourcebook Project, 1974), p. G2–43.

Page 17 "It seems to me": The Complete Books of Charles Fort by Charles Fort (New York: Dover, 1974), pp. 82–83.

Page 22 "things from the times": *The Complete Books of Charles Fort*, p. 91.

Page 23 "the discharge of": *Undaunted Courage: Meriwether Lewis, Thomas Jefferson, and the Opening of the American West* by Stephen E. Ambrose (New York: Simon & Schuster, 1996), p. 247.

Page 24 "the Indian god": *Strange Phenomena*, p. G1–216.

Page 26 "I used to play": "Trouble in Taos" by Anita Baskin, *Omni*, October 1993, p. 115.

Page 26 "a clear suggestion": *Atlas of the Supernatural* by Derek and Julia Parker (New York: Prentice Hall, 1990), p. 78.

Page 31 "in the air": *Appearances and Disappearances: Strange Comings and Goings from the Bermuda Triangle to the Mary Celeste* edited by Peter Brookesmith (Secaucus, NJ: Chartwell, 1989), p. 6.

Page 31 "Good God": *Appearances and Disappearances*, p. 34.

Page 33 "Was somebody collecting": *The Complete Books of Charles Fort*, p. 847.

Page 34 "garments of strange color": *Encyclopedia of Strange and Unexplained Physical Phenomena* by Jerome Clark (Detroit: Gale Research, 1993), p. 133.

Page 36 "so overwhelmed": *Encyclopedia of Strange and Unexplained Physical Phenomena*, p. 133.

Page 38 "some of the people": *Appearances and Disappearances*, p. 7.

Page 48 "full of vivacity": *Mysteries of the Unexplained*, p. 43.

Page 60 "a kind of helmet": Strange Stories, Amazing Facts by the Editors of *Reader's Digest* (Pleasantville, NY: Reader's Digest, 1976), p. 358.

Page 60 "huge shadow" and "just melted away": *Encyclopedia of Strange and Unexplained Physical Phenomena*, p. 299.

Page 61 "As might be": *This Baffling World* by John Godwin (New York: Hart, 1968), p. 77.

Page 62 "mournful and awful": *Bizarre Phenomena*, p. 62.

Page 65 "which looked like" and "the squeak": *Encyclopedia of Strange and Unexplained Physical Phenomena*, p. 229.

Page 65 "I've never had": *Mysteries of the Unexplained*, p. 165.

Page 70 "Many scientists take": *Atlas of the Supernatural*, p. 8.

Page 70 "The most beautiful": *Mysteries of the Unexplained*, p. 7.

About the Author

Gary L. Blackwood is a novelist and playwright who specializes in historical topics. His interest in the Unexplained goes back to his childhood, when he heard his father tell a story about meeting a ghost on a lonely country road.

Though he has yet to see a single UFO or ghost, a glimpse of the future or a past life, the author is keeping his eyes and his mind open. Gary lives in Missouri with his wife and two children.